VIRUSES

VIRUSES

HOWARD AND MARGERY FACKLAM

TWENTY-FIRST CENTURY BOOKS

A DIVISION OF HENRY HOLT AND COMPANY

NEW YORK

Twenty-First Century Books
A Division of Henry Holt and Company, Inc.
115 West 18th Street
New York, NY 10011

Henry Holt ® and colophon are trademarks of
Henry Holt and Company, Inc.
Publishers since 1866

Published in Canada by Fitzhenry & Whiteside Ltd.
195 Allstate Parkway, Markham, Ontario L3R 4T8

Library of Congress Cataloging-in-Publication Data
Facklam, Howard.
    Viruses / Howard and Margery Facklam. — 1st ed.
        p. cm. — (Invaders)
    Includes index.
    1. Viruses—Juvenile literature. 2. Virus diseases—Juvenile litera-
ture. [1. Viruses. 2. Virus diseases. 3. Diseases.] I. Facklam, Margery.
II. Title. III. Series.
    QR365.F33 1994
    576'64—dc20   94–25429
                                                                    CIP
                                                                     AC
ISBN 0–8050–2856–0
First Edition 1994
Printed in Mexico
All first editions are printed on acid–free paper ∞.
10 9 8 7 6 5 4 3 2

Photo Credits
pp. 8, 10, 34 (inset): A. B. Dowsett/SPL/Photo Researchers, Inc.; p. 12:
Courtesy of the Carolina Biological Supply; p. 15: John D.
Cunningham/Visuals Unlimited; p. 17: Jack Fields/Science Source/Photo
Researchers, Inc.; p. 19: Courtesy of the Cold Springs Harbor Laboratory;
p. 20: Lee D. Simon/Science Source/Photo Researchers, Inc.; p. 23: World
Health Organization/Peter Arnold, Inc.; p. 25: J. Phipps/The Bettmann
Archive; pp. 27, 34: The Bettmann Archive; p. 27 (inset):
Tektoff–RM/CNRI/SPL/Science Source/Photo Researchers, Inc.; p. 32:
Richard Walters/Visuals Unlimited; p. 36: Stock Montage, Inc.; p. 38:
NIH/R. Feldman/Visuals Unlimited; p. 39: R. Dourmashkin/SPL/Science
Source/Photo Researchers, Inc.; p. 43: NIBSC/SPL/Science
Source/Photo Researchers, Inc.; p. 46: Jim Levitt/Impact Visuals; p. 46
(inset): Eddie Adams/Sygma; p. 49: Kerry T. Givens/Tom Stack and
Associates; p. 51: David M. Dennis/Tom Stack and Associates; p. 52:
Courtesy of the U.S. Department of Agriculture; p. 57: Liaison
International.

CONTENTS

1
VIRUSES AND OUR DEFENSES

You have a virus right now! Although you may feel healthy and fit, there are viruses lurking in your body. They are the invisible, ever present invaders of every animal and plant. No living thing is free of viruses, but we do not become aware of them until they cause trouble.

No one knows how long viruses have been around. Scientists think they may have been here since the beginnings of life on earth, and it is likely they infected the dinosaurs. Scientists are quite sure, however, that viruses were causing diseases in humans at least 3,000 years ago. When scientists opened ancient tombs in Egypt, they found mummies pockmarked with the telltale scars of smallpox, which is caused by a virus. Other mummies were found with shriveled legs or arms. They probably had poliomyelitis, another disease caused by a virus.

We don't know how many different viruses there are, and scientists cannot even agree on exactly what they are. Just the word *virus* makes us think of diseases like AIDS, flu, rabies, mumps, measles, and the common cold. Distemper in dogs, leukemia in cats, and hoof-and-mouth disease in cattle are caused by viruses. Plant diseases by the hundreds are triggered by viruses, and even the tiniest bacterium is not safe from these even tinier invaders.

Most viruses are so small they can't be seen through an ordinary microscope. In Scotland in 1887, John Buist, a surgeon and bacteriologist, was probably the first person to see a virus. He had taken some fluid from a smallpox sore of a patient and put it under his microscope. He saw tiny reddish

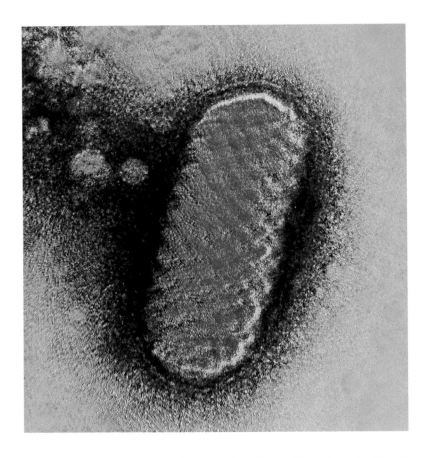

An electron-microscope picture of a virus. The virus is identified by its bricklike rectangular shape and fuzzy "ball of wool" appearance.

dots in the fluid, but he had no idea he was looking at what we now call viruses. The smallpox virus is one of the largest—1/100,000 inch in diameter, about one-fourth the size of any bacterium. More than 500 flu viruses could fit on the point of a pin, and flu viruses are medium sized. Other viruses are so small that a million or more could fit inside a single letter *o* on this page.

Since the invention of the electron microscope, which can enlarge things more than 100,000 times, scientists have been able to identify different viruses by their shapes. Some viruses are long, thin rods. Others look like soft, fluffy cotton balls. Still others are twenty-sided crystals. One kind of virus looks like a six-sided bullet, and another like a mace, which is an ancient war club with a spiked ball on top of the handle.

Are these tiny organisms alive? Scientists today still debate this question. Living things grow, reproduce, and use food for energy. A virus can't do any of these things unless it is inside a living cell. Outside a cell, a virus does nothing. It remains dormant, or inactive. It appears to be just a nonliving bunch of chemicals that can be frozen or crystallized with no harmful effects. A virus can survive for years, even centuries, in this inactive state. It may even float around in space on specks of dust. But once inside a living cell, a virus becomes active. Using the cell's machinery to make energy, the virus creates more viruses. Like some kind of science fiction alien, the invading virus seems to turn the cell against itself. Early researchers were so mystified by viruses that one called them "positively unnatural."

Scientists now define a virus as an extremely small, simple, infectious organism that can grow and duplicate itself only in a living cell. A typical virus is made up of DNA (deoxyribonucleic acid) or RNA (ribonucleic acid) surrounded by a protein coat. Both DNA and RNA are molecules that contain genetic information in the form of a code.

So in effect, a virus is a packet of coded information in a protective capsule.

Since disease viruses are everywhere, why aren't we sick all the time? The answer lies in the human body's amaz-

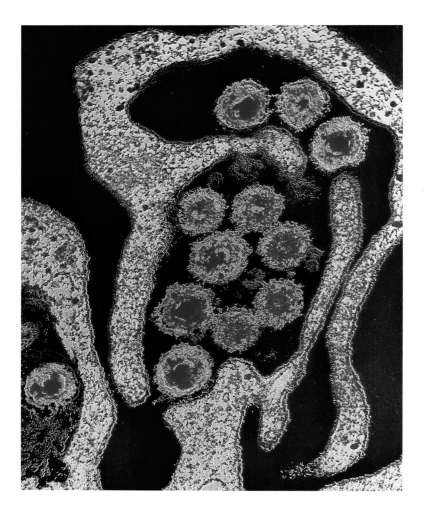

Viruses (red particles) within a cell, each showing a thick protein coat and darker red core of DNA. These viruses cause a childhood disease characterized by a rose-colored skin rash.

ing system of protection. The body's first line of defense is its fortress of skin, which is made up of a layer of dead, dry cells that covers closely packed living cells. If this barrier is not broken—scratched, cut, or torn—viruses are kept out.

Even the natural openings in this skin fortress are protected. Saliva and tears are natural antiseptics that protect the mouth and eyes from viruses. The mucus lining in the nose and mouth traps viruses like sticky flypaper. Some organisms are destroyed by chemicals in the mucus. In the bronchial tubes, thousands of tiny hairs called cilia beat upward to sweep mucus-trapped viruses up into the throat where they are swallowed. Most viruses can't survive the acid they then encounter in the stomach.

When viruses do slip past this first line of defense, the body turns on its biggest weapon—the immune system. This is an army of trillions of soldiers, the white cells. Some white cells patrol the bloodstream and body tissues. Others are stationed in the tonsils, liver, spleen, and lymph nodes. The lymph nodes are outposts at strategic spots in the neck, chest, groin, and armpits. During an infection, the white cells in the lymph nodes become active, which causes the lymph nodes to swell. This is why a doctor checks a patient for signs of a viral infection by feeling for swollen lymph nodes.

About two trillion white cells called lymphocytes prowl the bloodstream looking for unfamiliar objects such as viruses, bacteria, and parasites. Special lymphocytes called B cells are programmed in the bone marrow to recognize these foreign invaders. When an invader is discovered, the B cells start making antibodies to destroy it. Antibodies are custom-made chemicals that destroy only one particular invader. If, for example, the chicken pox virus invades the body, the B cells make only chicken pox antibodies. The chicken pox antibodies will not work against any other virus.

It takes B cells five to seven days to make enough anti-

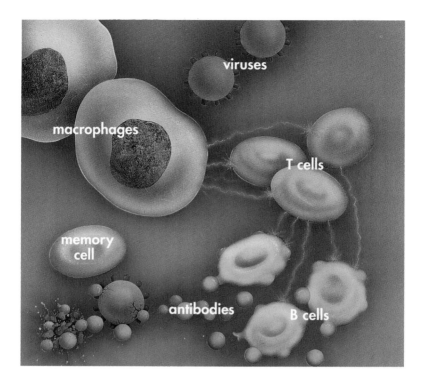

The human immune system reacting to a viral invasion. Macrophages, which are large phagocytes, try to engulf the viruses as well as send chemical signals to T cells. T cells multiply and send chemical signals to B cells, which multiply and produce other B cells specifically matched to the invading viruses. These B cells produce antibodies to the viruses. When the antibodies have done their job, T cells signal B cells to stop multiplying and producing antibodies. A few memory cells remain in the blood in case the same viruses invade the body again.

bodies to fight a virus. After a person has been infected by the chicken pox virus, he or she will be sick for about a week before enough antibodies are produced to take over the virus. Then the person will start to get better.

Soon after viruses invade a body they move into their specific target cells. Once hidden in those cells, antibodies cannot identify and destroy the viruses. So another line of defense is called in—the T cells. T cells are lymphocytes that are programmed in the thymus, a small gland in the chest under the breastbone. Killer T cells find infected cells and uncover the viruses so antibodies can destroy them. Killer T cells also release chemicals that attract another kind of white cells called phagocytes. Phagocyte means "cell eater." Phagocytes engulf and digest the viruses uncovered by killer T cells. Still other T cells, called the helper T cells, direct and control the entire attack of the immune system.

Other body cells are not completely defenseless against invaders. When attacked by a virus, any cell will release a chemical called interferon, which warns nearby cells of a virus in the neighborhood. Tiny amounts of interferon inhibit a virus's ability to make more viruses.

Once someone has recovered from a disease like mumps or scarlet fever, she or he generally does not get the disease again because B cells and T cells have made memory cells. When a mumps virus enters the body of a person who has had mumps, a memory cell recognizes it as a virus that has been there before. There is no five-to-seven day delay to start antibody production. With memory cells, antibodies are produced so fast the virus doesn't have a chance to start its attack. And memory cells can last for years, even a lifetime.

A vaccine made of killed or weakened viruses works because it stimulates the production of antibodies and memory cells in the body without causing the disease. After receiving a vaccine, a person is immune to the disease because the memory cells will mount an instant attack against the virus if it invades the body.

The war between a person's immune system and foreign invaders is constant. When the immune system wins, the invaders are killed. When the invaders win, the person dies.

13

2
HOW VIRUSES WORK

Scientific discoveries are often the result of a slow, steady accumulation of information. Each scientist builds on the work of others. John Buist first saw a virus in 1887 and didn't know what it was. In 1892, a Russian botanist, Dimitry Ivanovski, filtered a virus, but he didn't know what it was either. But both scientists were adding to the facts about these unnamed organisms.

Ivanovski was trying to find the cause of a disease that was destroying valuable tobacco crops in Russia. It was called tobacco mosaic disease because of the mottled, or mosaic, pattern made on the leaves by spots of light, healthy tissue and dark, diseased tissue. Ivanovski collected the juice from crushed and squeezed infected tobacco leaves. He passed it through a filter with pores small enough to trap bacteria because at the time, bacteria were the smallest organisms known. When Ivanovski rubbed the filtered juice on healthy tobacco leaves, the plants became infected. This meant that whatever was causing the disease was so small it passed through the filter. But when Ivanovski looked at the juice under the microscope, he did not see any bacteria. He decided that whatever caused tobacco mosaic disease must be a poison made by the bacteria that was dissolved in the juice.

Leaves showing the mottled color and wrinkled texture caused by the tobacco mosaic virus. Before the virus was identified, Ivanovski determined these three things about the cause of tobacco mosaic disease: it was smaller than a bacterium, it was contagious, and it multiplied in the host plant.

Dutch botanist, Martinus Willem Beijerinck, was also interested in finding the cause of tobacco mosaic disease. In the early 1880s, he had looked for a bacterium, but found none. In 1895 he tried again. He carried out experiments similar to Ivanovski's, although he did not know of the other scientist's work. Beijerinck knew the disease was not caused by a poison because a healthy plant growing next to, but not touching, a diseased plant could become infected. Whatever the cause, he knew it was something that grew and multiplied. He named this disease-causing thing a filterable virus.

About the same time, in the late 1800s, an epidemic of hoof-and-mouth disease was killing cattle in Germany, and two researchers, Friedrich Loeffler and Paul Frosch, were

15

looking for the cause. They collected pus from sores on infected cattle. When they passed the pus through a filter, they did not find any bacteria in it. But when they injected healthy cattle with this filtered material, the cattle came down with hoof-and-mouth disease. Here was another disease caused by a filterable virus, the first one found in animals.

Yellow fever was the first human disease found to be caused by one of these filterable viruses. In 1900, when Major Walter Reed was sent to Cuba to study yellow fever, the disease was thought to be caused by bacteria. Although Major Reed could not see what caused the disease, he found a filterable virus in the *Aedes* mosquitoes that carried it.

Fifteen years later, a British bacteriologist, Frederick Twort, found another filterable virus, one that infects and kills bacteria. So by 1915, scientists had found something that could not be seen and could not be grown in a laboratory, but that could pass through the finest filter and could cause diseases in plants, animals, humans, and bacteria.

The nature of viruses was still a mystery in 1932 when a 28-year-old biochemist, Wendell Stanley, started to work on the cause of tobacco mosaic disease. At the Rockefeller Institute's plant pathology lab in Princeton, New Jersey, Stanley raised tobacco in test fields and greenhouses. He infected his crop of healthy plants by rubbing the leaves with juice taken from infected plants. When he had harvested more than a ton of infected plants, he ran them through a powerful meat grinder. He caught the pulp in five-gallon pails and then drained the pulp in large gauze bags to collect the juice. From his buckets and buckets of infected juice, Stanley still had to get rid of everything but the pure virus. So he filtered, evaporated, and precipitated the juice over and over again until it turned from a rich brown to yellow. Finally he was left with a small flask of clear juice, which was hundreds of times more potent than the juice he started with.

Stanley rubbed this juice onto the leaves of a healthy tobacco plant. The leaves quickly became mottled and the plant died.

Stanley was quite sure the virus was a protein, so he put the juice through the procedures used to crystallize a protein. From more than a ton of infected tobacco leaves, Stanley finally had one teaspoon of white crystals. Under a microscope, the crystals looked like long, thin needles, and each crystal was made up of millions of individual viruses. These, at last, were pure tobacco mosaic viruses. In 1935, after three years of hard work, Stanley read a headline in the *New York Times* announcing his discovery: "Crystals Isolated at Princeton Believed Unseen Disease Virus."

Dr. Wendell Stanley, the first person to form crystals from a microorganism: the tobacco mosaic virus. For this work, Stanley shared the 1946 Nobel Prize in chemistry.

Obtaining the crystals of a virus was important, but it took many more years of research before scientists figured out how viruses worked. For one thing, they needed an inexpensive but plentiful supply of viruses to study. The yellow fever virus had been grown in mice, and other viruses had been grown in rabbits. But using live animals was too dangerous. Too many things could happen that the scientists could not control. The animals' immune systems might destroy the viruses, the animals might get sick and die, or the experimental viruses might mix with viruses already in the animals and produce false data. In 1931, however, researchers found nature's perfect, inexpensive experimental container—an egg. Viruses grew and multiplied when injected into fertilized hen eggs. Scientists also learned how to grow animal and human cells in test tubes. These cells were then inoculated with viruses grown in eggs to see the effects of viral infections on different kinds of cells.

During the 1940s and 1950s, a group of microbiologists, chemists, and physicists from all over the world met during the summers at a laboratory in Cold Spring Harbor, New York, to study a unique kind of virus called a bacteriophage. Bacteriophage means "bacteria eater," and that is exactly what these viruses do. They live only in bacteria. These scientists, who became known as the Phage Group, unraveled many of the mysteries of how a virus works in a cell.

Using an electron microscope, scientists could see a virus's shape, but they could not see what it was made of or how it was put together. That required a technique called X-ray crystallography, in which high-powered X rays are used to produce hundreds of images of a crystallized virus. The data from the X-ray images is fed into a computer. The computer then produces a picture of the complete atomic make-up of the virus.

Once a virus enters a specific plant or animal, it infects

The Phage Group, 1949. Much of the information we have today about viruses and their reproduction is based on the work of these scientists and others in the group.

only certain cells. In humans, for example, the polio virus infects stomach cells first. Then it grows and multiplies and spreads to the nervous system. All the different cold viruses infect only the cells in the throat and nose. And the hepatitis virus infects only the cells of the liver.

Using X-ray crystallography pictures of viruses, scientists figured out how the molecules on the outer coat of a virus allow the virus to enter and infect only specific cells. Every cell is surrounded by a membrane made of protein and fat molecules. Some of these protein molecules have specific shapes that act as receptor, or landing, sites. In order to land on one of these receptor sites, a substance must have a shape that matches the landing site. It must fit like a piece of a puzzle or a key in a lock. All the materials that must enter a cell for it to grow, reproduce, and carry out its function in the body arrive at and fit into these receptor sites. If a virus fits into a receptor site, it, too, can enter the cell. The hepatitis B virus is the right shape to enter liver cells. The AIDS virus has a shape that allows it to enter certain kinds of white cells.

Once a virus attaches itself to a receptor site, it enters the cell. One kind of virus, for example, attaches itself to a receptor site with its long, spidery legs and forces its genetic material into the cell through a taillike tube. Other viruses almost seem to be invited into a cell. When one of these viruses fits into a receptor site, the cell is fooled into taking it in as though it were one of the cell's regular suppliers of food or fuel.

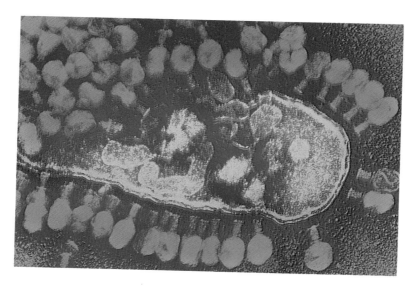

A bacteriophage attacking a bacterial cell. The tails of many of the bacteriophages have contracted, injecting the DNA in their heads into the cell.

The genetic material of an invading virus literally hijacks the cell's machinery. It forces the cell to start making virus DNA or RNA instead of its own. Every living cell contains DNA, which holds complete instructions for making exact copies of that cell or an entire organism. When a virus takes over, the cell no longer works for itself. It duplicates virus DNA or RNA and protein coats for these new viruses. When the new viruses break out of the cell, they destroy the cell before moving on to infect other cells. Some kinds of viruses quietly slip out, leaving the cell to continue making viruses for several more hours before it is destroyed.

Each virus has a unique pattern of action. The chicken pox virus usually attacks children, causing a mild disease. But the virus stays hidden in the child's body and may attack again 40 or 50 years later in the form of a painful disease called shingles. Cold sores or fever blisters are caused by a virus that remains in the body and only becomes active when the person's resistance is low. The AIDS virus can remain inactive for months or years before it becomes active and produces symptoms.

What triggers an inactive virus into action? The answer is still a mystery, although it seems that a virus responds to some signal. It could be a person's lowered resistance, or stress, or chemicals in the air we breathe. Or it could be something a person eats or drinks, or simply the process of aging.

SMALLPOX
AND RABIES

Smallpox is the only disease that has ever been completely conquered. But finding a way to control this disease was a long battle against one of the world's most deadly plagues, which killed millions and millions of people. The smallpox virus produces a rash on the body similar to chicken pox. But chicken pox marks disappear. Smallpox sores leave permanent, disfiguring scars all over the body, especially on the face and even in the mouth. People who survived the disease were often blind. Death was terrible as the pox literally rotted away the body.

Smallpox was first described in China in 1122 B.C., and it left its mark in ancient Egypt, too. The mummified head of King Ramses V shows evidence of scarring from smallpox. Historians think smallpox was carried to Europe from Asia and Africa during the Crusades in the twelfth and thirteenth centuries. In Europe in the 1700s, probably 95 percent of the population had smallpox at some time. One in every ten people died, and half of them were children.

When Hernando Cortés sailed from Spain to Mexico in 1519, he conquered the Aztec Empire with 508 soldiers and a silent killer called smallpox. The virus did not exist in the New World, and the Aztecs had no resistance or antibodies to

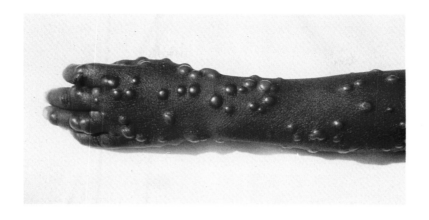

Sores on the arm of a person suffering from smallpox. The smallpox virus is transmitted by droplets of coughed up saliva and mucus or by pus from the skin sores of infected people.

this new disease. Within two years of Cortés's arrival, about four million Aztecs died from smallpox. When early settlers arrived in North America, smallpox came with them. It caused more deaths among Native Americans than all the wars with them. And as recently as 1967, the smallpox virus was the cause of two million deaths worldwide.

As early as the eleventh century, the Chinese and people in other Asian countries used a method called ingrafting to combat smallpox. Having noticed that people who survived a bout of smallpox seldom got the disease again, someone was brave enough to try a crude kind of vaccination. Pus taken from a person who had a mild case of smallpox was transferred to a scratch in the arm of a healthy person. The healthy person usually developed mild symptoms of smallpox, but quickly recovered and never got smallpox again.

When Lady Mary Wortley Montagu, the wife of the British ambassador, was living in Turkey in 1716, she saw these crude inoculations. She decided to take a chance and have her three-year-old son inoculated. That inoculation worked, and when Lady Mary returned to England, she tried to convince doctors to use this procedure. They wanted no part of it. So Lady Mary went to the Prince of Wales, and he made it possible for her to conduct an experiment at Newgate Prison. Six convicted felons were promised pardons if they would volunteer for inoculations. When all the prisoners survived the inoculations and did not get smallpox, King George I was so impressed he had his two grandchildren inoculated, too. Even though these first inoculations were successful, they were dangerous, and they did not become common practice. So years went by with the threat of smallpox remaining.

In his practice as a country doctor, Edward Jenner had noticed that dairymaids, young women who milked cows, sometimes became infected with cowpox. This disease caused sores on a cow's udder. In humans, cowpox was a mild disease that caused only a few sores on the hands, which quickly healed. But the important thing Jenner realized was that once the dairymaids had been infected with cowpox, they did not get smallpox.

In May 1796, Jenner began an incredible experiment. He took fluid from fresh cowpox sores on the fingers of a dairymaid named Sarah Nelmes and used it to inoculate an eight-year-old boy, James Phipps. In the next few days, James developed a slight fever and a small sore, but he did not get cowpox or smallpox. By 1800, more than 100,000 people had been made immune to smallpox with this cowpox inoculation. A way had been found to conquer the disease even though no one at the time knew what caused it or how the inoculations worked.

Between 1967 and 1976, the World Health Organization carried out a worldwide program of vaccinations to wipe out smallpox, and in 1977, smallpox became the only disease ever

Edward Jenner vaccinating James Phipps. Jenner was the first person to scientifically demonstrate that the technique of vaccination could be used to protect against a disease.

officially eliminated. All that is left of the disease are 600 test tubes of smallpox viruses, frozen in liquid nitrogen and stored in heavily guarded laboratories—400 in Atlanta, Georgia, and 200 in Moscow, Russia. The World Health Organization believes there is a risk in keeping these lethal viruses. There is always a chance of an accidental release of the viruses, or the viruses might be stolen and used by terrorists. The organization asked both the United States and

Russia to flip a switch on December 31, 1993, that would heat up the test tubes and destroy the viruses. Scientists the world over, however, were opposed to this destruction. Some argued that keeping the virus was worth the risk because live smallpox viruses are a valuable library of information. One scientist said, "Smallpox is still a mystery, we don't even know how it kills." Other scientists believed further study and a greater understanding of the smallpox virus might help in fighting other viral diseases, and still others were opposed to deliberately destroying an entire species. Because of such opposition, the destruction of the stored smallpox viruses was postponed. In May 1995, the World Health Organization will make a final decision about what to do with the viruses.

Rabies is another viral disease for which a vaccine was discovered long before scientists knew which organism caused the disease. Rabies infects only mammals and is carried only by mammals. A hundred years ago, some of the major carriers of rabies were domestic animals like dogs and cats. Today, vaccination campaigns have controlled rabies in these animals, but the disease has increased in wild animals.

On a sunny July afternoon in France in 1885, nine-year-old Joseph Meister was attacked by a rabid dog. In terror, he had thrown up his hands to protect his face. But by the time the dog was driven off, Joseph had fourteen deep bites on his hands, arms, and legs. He was sure to get rabies. At the time, there was no known way to save him from this horrible and always fatal disease.

Over the years, all kinds of desperate treatments for rabies had been tried. There were people who believed eating the liver from a rabid dog would cure the disease. Others thought rabies could be cured by eating a paste made from the eyes of a crayfish. Some said the infection could be stopped if the tissues around the wound that had been in contact with the dog's saliva were destroyed. So rabies wounds were drenched with acid or burned with a red-hot iron. Still another method advised sprinkling the wound with gunpowder and lighting it. If people managed to live through such ghastly treatments, they died from rabies anyway.

Desperate to save her son, Joseph Meister's mother took him to Paris to see Louis Pasteur. Pasteur was a scientist who had become famous for his brilliant discoveries, such as

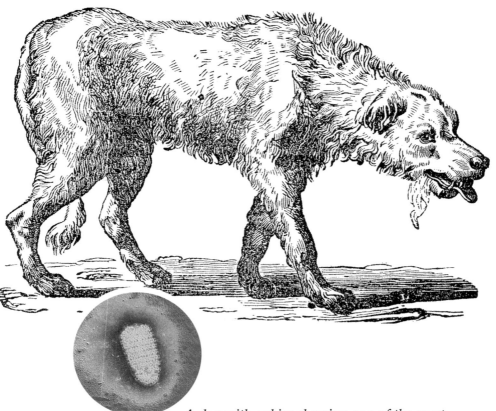

A dog with rabies showing one of the symptoms of the disease, extreme salivation. Inset: The bullet-shaped virus that causes rabies. The rabies virus is transmitted to humans in an animal's saliva when it bites.

a way to destroy bacteria in milk, which we call pasteurization. He had saved the French silk industry by finding the tiny parasite that was infecting silkworms. Pasteur had also found the germs that caused cholera in chickens and anthrax in sheep, and he used Jenner's techniques to make vaccines against these diseases.

After he was successful in making two vaccines for animal diseases, Pasteur began experiments to find a vaccine for rabies. He had been studying rabies for two years when Mrs. Meister brought Joseph to see him. Pasteur had made an experimental vaccine that protected dogs from rabies, but he had not tried it on humans. He hadn't been able to see the rabies "germ" under his microscope, and he didn't know it was a virus. All Pasteur knew was that vaccines made of weakened germs worked against other diseases, so a similar vaccine ought to work against rabies.

Pasteur was fearful of giving his vaccine to Joseph. Was it weak enough? Or was it too weak? Doctors had said Joseph's wounds were so deep he surely was infected with rabies and would die. Mrs. Meister must have felt she had no choice. Pasteur's vaccine was the boy's only chance. So despite his doubts, Pasteur gave Joseph a first injection of a very weak vaccine. The next day he injected a vaccine that was a little stronger, and each day for 14 days, he injected a stronger and stronger vaccine. On the last day, the vaccine was full strength, and Joseph Meister became the first human to survive rabies.

Today the treatment for rabies is shorter and less painful, but rabies is still the terrible disease it was in Pasteur's time. We are in the midst of an epidemic of rabies now. In 1988, there were 4,600 confirmed cases of rabies in animals in the United States. By 1993, there were 9,498 cases, and New York State led the list with 2,747 rabid animals reported. According to one health official,

"Confirmed cases of rabies are just the tip of the iceberg because there are far more diseased animals out there that just don't meet with people."

The rabies virus moves through the body in the nervous system, not the bloodstream. Therefore, the immune system is not involved, antibodies are not made to fight off the virus, and the disease cannot be detected while it is incubating. By the time symptoms appear, from a month or up to two years after infection, it is too late for treatment to help. Once the rabies virus gets to the brain, death is certain. Treatment must begin as soon as a person becomes aware of being infected, before symptoms appear.

In July 1993, 12-year-old Kelly Ahrendt of Mamakating, New York, was not as lucky as Joseph Meister in 1885. Kelly died of rabies, without anyone ever knowing she had the disease. After her death, tests on Kelly's body turned up a strain of rabies virus usually found in bats. No one knows for sure how Kelly got rabies. She had not been bitten by an animal, but a bite or scratch is not always necessary. She may have found a dead bat, picked it up, and become infected that way. Two people are known to have picked up rabies in caves just by breathing air contaminated by rabid bats.

To protect yourself from rabies, follow some simple rules. Make sure pets have been vaccinated against rabies. Keep away from any animal that acts unnaturally—an overly tame raccoon, which usually feeds at night, wandering around during the day, for example. Even though you want to help a wild animal that may seem sick or hungry, don't! Instead, call the police or the conservation department. If you are bitten or scratched, wash the wound well and get medical help immediately. And notify the police to try to catch the animal so it can be tested for rabies.

YELLOW FEVER AND POLIO

Yellow fever was the third viral disease conquered by a vaccine before anyone had seen a virus. The name of this ancient disease comes from some of its symptoms: yellow eyes and skin. The virus attacks the liver, which causes this yellow coloring, called jaundice. More severe liver damage causes death.

For centuries, yellow fever was such a common disease in Africa that many people developed resistance to it. Children, especially, often had mild infections of yellow fever that left them immune to further attacks. But people in other parts of the world did not have this resistance, and attacks of yellow fever were more severe, often fatal. Trading ships from Africa probably carried the disease to Europe. In 1857, an epidemic of yellow fever killed 6,000 people in the port city of Lisbon, Portugal. British soldiers called the disease "yellow jack" because quarantine flags were flown on ships below the Union Jack (British flag) to warn others of the disease.

Trading ships from Spain, Portugal, and Africa then carried yellow fever to the Americas. The French gave up on building the Panama Canal in 1889 because more than 20,000 laborers had died of yellow fever and malaria.

Yellow fever moved from Central America into the

southern United States and up the coast to Baltimore, New York City, and Boston. One year an epidemic of yellow fever killed 13,000 people in the Mississippi valley. Wherever yellow fever had struck, it was common to see clouds of smoke from the burning of clothes, blankets, and bedding used by patients who had died. It was thought such items became infected and spread the disease.

Dr. Carlos Finlay, who practiced medicine in Cuba, was certain that mosquitoes carried yellow fever. But when he published the results of his experiments in 1886, other scientists said he had not shown real proof, and his ideas were ignored for almost 15 years.

In 1900, Major Walter Reed was sent to the U.S. military post in Havana, Cuba, where several soldiers had died from yellow fever. Dr. Finlay convinced Major Reed to study the mosquito as the carrier of the disease. James Carroll, a doctor on Reed's staff, volunteered to let an infected mosquito bite him. Dr. Carroll became sick with yellow fever, but he recovered. Major Reed then recruited more volunteers for a series of controlled experiments to prove that mosquitoes, and not bedding, bacteria, or polluted air, carried the disease.

The carrier of yellow fever turned out to be the female *Aedes* mosquito, a species that breeds in puddles and containers of water around cities and farms. Before she lays her eggs, the female mosquito needs a blood meal. When she drinks the blood of a person infected with yellow fever, the mosquito drinks in the virus, too. For 12 days the virus reproduces within the mosquito and travels to its salivary glands. The virus is then passed in the insect's saliva to the next person the mosquito bites.

People learned to control the mosquitoes by draining ditches and ponds where they live and by putting screens on windows. But there was no miracle cure for yellow fever. Although Major Reed had not seen the actual virus, all evi-

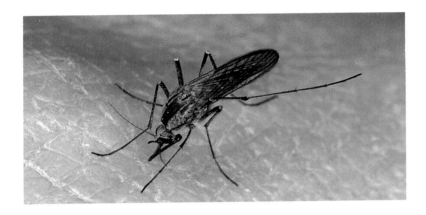

The female Aedes *mosquito, carrier of the yellow fever virus, feeding on human blood. Yellow fever begins suddenly three to five days after a person has been bitten by an infected mosquito. The disease can range from mild to severe.*

dence pointed to one of the filterable viruses as the cause of yellow fever.

In the 1920s, a young South African, Max Theiler, arrived at Harvard University Medical Center to work on a vaccine against yellow fever. His plan was to make the vaccine from a weakened form of the virus as Jenner and Pasteur had done. But to do this, Theiler needed to grow a crop of the virus. He found that if he injected blood from a monkey infected with yellow fever into mice, he could pass the virus to the mice. The mice didn't get the disease. But the virus lived and multiplied in the cells of the mice, and those viruses could be passed on to other mice. Theiler also found that every time he passed it to another mouse, the virus became weaker. After passing the virus through many mice, Theiler injected the weakened virus into a monkey. The monkey came down with a light case of yellow fever and then recovered in a few days, so Theiler knew he had found the weakened virus for a vaccine. When the vaccine was tested on humans, it caused a slight fever for two or three days. But it also made the people completely immune to yellow fever.

The parents of children who grew up in the first half of the twentieth century were terrified when a child complained of chills or a stiff neck. If children had fevers or aching legs, arms, or backs, they were rushed to a doctor because everyone was afraid of poliomyelitis. Commonly called polio, the disease was also known as infantile paralysis because it could leave a child with paralyzed arms or legs. When the paralysis struck the nerves of the chest, the child couldn't breathe and had to be placed in an iron lung, a machine that breathed for the patient.

No one knew what caused polio or how it was spread. Parents were frightened, and during epidemics children were kept home, away from beaches, movie theaters, and other crowded places where they might catch the disease. The first polio epidemic in the United States, in the summer of 1916, left 27,000 children paralyzed and 6,000 dead. In 1937, an epidemic struck in Toronto, Canada. Based on the theory that the polio germ entered the body through the nose, thousands of Canadian children had their noses sprayed with zinc oxide to keep the germs from getting in. The treatment did not work, and some children lost their sense of smell. But people were willing to try anything.

We now know polio is caused by a virus that enters the body through the mouth. It infects and multiplies in cells of the stomach and intestines, and produces flulike symptoms in the first week. If the body doesn't conquer the virus at that point, the virus moves on to the central nervous system. If it attacks the spinal cord, the virus injures nerves that send messages to the muscles. When the muscles do not get messages, they cannot move. They are paralyzed. If the nerves are only damaged, they often recover in six months to a year,

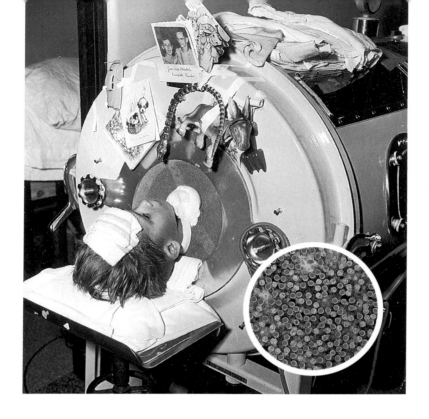

A child recovering from polio in an iron lung. Inset: Particles of the virus that causes polio. There are three types of polio virus, only one of which is the cause of most polio epidemics.

and the patient recovers without paralysis. But if the virus kills the nerves, the paralysis is permanent.

There was and is no cure for polio. The only hope was prevention in the form of a vaccine. After many years of research, two scientists came up with two different vaccines. One was made from a killed virus and one was made from a weakened virus. A killed virus is safe because it cannot give a person the disease, and it will give immunity to most people. A weakened virus always gives immunity, but there is also the chance the virus isn't weak enough and that it might cause the disease, too.

Dr. Jonas Salk created a killed virus vaccine because he

believed a weakened virus could never be 100 percent safe. In 1952, after he had made a vaccine that was safe in monkeys and gave them immunity to polio, Salk was ready to test the vaccine on humans. He vaccinated 45 children who had once had polio because he knew they would have built up a natural immunity to the disease. The children would be safe even if the vaccine itself proved to be harmful. The tests showed the vaccine to be safe in humans. The tests also proved that the children had not picked up any live polio viruses and that their immunity to polio increased.

As many scientists in the past had done, Dr. Salk injected himself, his wife, and his three children with the vaccine before giving it to the general population. Neither Dr. Salk nor his family came down with polio, and tests showed they had developed immunity to the disease. No scientist today would be allowed to take such chances because medicines and drugs must go through years of testing by the manufacturers and the Food and Drug Administration before they can be tried on people.

Between 1940 and 1950 there had been a series of polio epidemics, and the public was anxious for a vaccine. A massive test of Dr. Salk's vaccine was scheduled for April 26, 1954, and expectations were high. First, second, and third graders from selected schools across the nation lined up to be vaccinated. Thousands of volunteers helped as 441,000 children were given the vaccine and 201,000 children were given a placebo. A placebo is a harmless substance that looks like the drug or medicine being tested. In this test, the placebo was a colored solution that looked like the vaccine. No one, except for a few people at the Polio Foundation, knew who was getting the vaccine and who was getting the placebo.

When the results of the test were announced, the public went wild. The vaccine had proved to be 94 percent effective.

Headline of the Chicago Daily News *announcing the success of the nationwide test of Dr. Jonas Salk's polio vaccine. At the time of the announcement, bells rang and fire engine sirens screamed across the nation, and people put up signs saying,* THANK YOU DR. SALK.

For the first time in years, parents relaxed. In 1955, a national campaign against polio was started. More than five million children were vaccinated by their family doctors or at clinics in schools and community centers.

During the time Dr. Salk was developing his killed virus vaccine, another scientist had been working on a weakened virus vaccine. Dr. Albert Sabin believed it would be cheaper, safer, and easier to give his vaccine because it didn't need to be injected. It could be eaten. After the Sabin vaccine was proved effective and approved for use in the United States in 1960, more than 70 million school children ate sugar cubes soaked in the weakened polio virus. And we have been using this vaccine ever since.

COLDS, FLU, AND AIDS

The ancient Greeks thought a runny nose due to a cold was waste material draining from the brain. In the twelfth century, the best treatment for a cold was soup made from a fat hen. During the Middle Ages in Europe, people believed that demons would rush in when bits of a person's soul were forced out during a sneeze. The habit of covering the mouth and nose when a person sneezed was not for courtesy or cleanliness, but a way of preventing the soul from leaving. Little did people realize how far that habit went toward keeping a cold from spreading. Cold viruses are spread widely in the tiny droplets of moisture from coughs and sneezes.

Using X-ray crystallography, researchers developed the first mapped, detailed, three-dimensional model of an animal virus in 1985. It was a cold virus. Scientists used an atom smasher and powerful X rays to produce hundreds of images of the virus crystal. The photographs were then broken down into six million bits of information and fed into a supercomputer. What scientists saw was a cold virus that looked like a soccer ball made of 20 closely fitted triangles.

Even with all this modern, high-tech equipment, scientists don't seem any closer to preventing colds than the ancient Greeks. About 300 different cold viruses have been

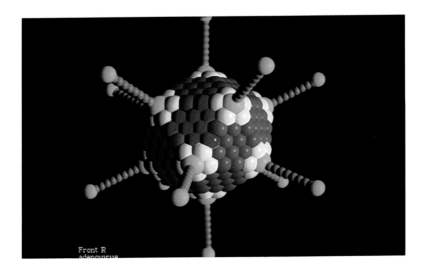

Computer-generated three-dimensional model of a cold virus. This cold virus belongs to a group of viruses that cause eye and respiratory tract infections.

identified, and each requires a different antibody to fight it. This is why you can get a cold this week, and two weeks later get another one. Even though your body may have developed antibodies to the first cold virus, they are of no use against the second cold virus. Because so many viruses are involved, many researchers doubt we will ever have a vaccine that prevents all colds.

If in addition to a stuffy, runny nose, you have a fever, ache all over, and seem to have trouble breathing, you probably do not have a cold. Most likely you have the flu, or influenza. Usually only small children get a fever with a cold, but a cold never goes into the lungs and does not cause breathing difficulty. The lungs are too warm for a cold virus to survive, but they are just fine for a flu virus. A cold may be unpleasant, but it is not serious. Flu, however, can be a more dangerous and sometimes fatal disease, especially for the elderly, chronically ill, or very young.

During the winter of 1918, half the people in the world had the flu, and almost 30 million people died. In the United States alone, more than half a million died. That bout of flu was one of the great epidemics in history. It was called the Spanish flu because it started in Spain and spread throughout Europe and across the Atlantic Ocean to North America. It was an extremely deadly virus that struck people down before they knew what hit them. It was said that if four people played cards together one evening, three of them would be dead by morning. One report told of a person who felt well enough to go to work one morning but died from the flu on the streetcar 15 minutes after leaving home. The only medi-

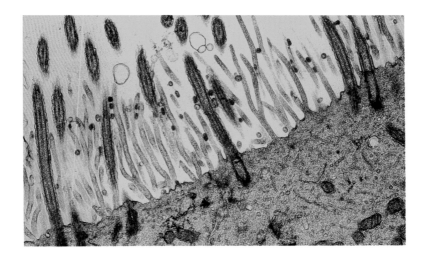

Flu viruses (tiny black dots) in the human windpipe. The viruses are filtering through the cilia (fingerlike projections), which line the windpipe and usually sweep it free of foreign particles. When too many viruses accumulate, the cilia become clogged, allowing the viruses to take hold.

cines available did nothing but keep a person comfortable for a while. There was not one drug to fight this virus, and no antibiotics to fight the pneumonia caused by bacteria that got into the lungs.

A flu virus is a quick-change artist. It can suddenly mutate, making a slight change in the genetic code that determines its outer protein coat. A change in the outer coat of a virus is like a man disguising himself with a mustache, different color hair, and different clothes. Just as the person would not be recognized by friends, the mutant virus is not recognized by the memory cells in the immune system. Antibodies made against last year's flu virus will be of no use against this year's mutant virus.

Every now and then a virus makes a major change that makes it far more dangerous. The Spanish flu was such a changed virus, and there have been two others since. In 1957, the Asian flu killed 80,000 people in the United States. It would have killed more, but by then we had antibiotics that prevented secondary bacterial infections. In 1968, about 28,000 people in the United States died from the Hong Kong flu. Some scientists predict we are due for another serious flu epidemic before the end of the twentieth century.

Another thing that makes flu viruses unusual is their ability to infect a wide range of domestic and wild animals. Flu viruses have been found in horses, pigs, cows, turkeys, ducks, and chickens. In 1980, 500 Atlantic harbor seals died from a virus closely related to human flu, and in 1986, dying whales that beached themselves on Cape Cod were found to be infected with a flu virus.

In Asia, and especially in southern China, it is common for farmers to keep fish and ducks in ponds that are fertilized with pig manure. Pigs come down with human flu, which they catch from the farmers who tend them. The pigs also catch bird, or avian, flu from the ducks. The pig is like a mixing

40

bowl for viruses, a place where the bird and human viruses can combine to form new strains of flu viruses. A new virus strain can then be caught by ducks and geese and carried during migration flights to all parts of the world. This pig–bird connection is one of the main sources of new flu viruses.

Because the flu virus mutates so frequently, a new flu vaccine must be made each year. Scientists cannot wait until winter to see what the new flu will be because there would not be time to make and distribute a new vaccine. As a result, scientists have to make educated guesses about what the next year's virus will be like, and then make a vaccine to fight it. Some researchers say that even though they have only a 50 percent chance of being right, the new vaccines are worthwhile.

Cold and flu viruses have been with us for centuries, but AIDS is new to the late twentieth century. Many scientists believe the AIDS virus started in Africa 50 to 100 years earlier when a virus in monkeys mutated. The virus jumped species to humans, probably when an infected monkey scratched or bit a human. The earliest recorded case of AIDS occurred in 1959. When stored, frozen blood samples taken from the victim were tested years later, scientists discovered the blood contained antibodies against the virus we now call HIV, proving the person had been infected with HIV. By the 1970s, this unidentified disease was sweeping through parts of Africa.

In the summer of 1981, a mysterious disease began to show up in Los Angeles and San Francisco. The patients all had severely weakened immune systems that left them with a variety of uncontrolled infections and tumors. Some of the infections were rare types not usually found in humans. It wasn't long before similar cases started to appear in New York City and Newark, New Jersey. By the end of 1981, about

150 cases of this strange disease had been reported, with 30 deaths. The same disease was showing up in Europe, too. Doctors suspected an unknown virus, and laboratories around the world began to search for it.

Almost at the same time, in the fall of 1982, two laboratories, the Pasteur Institute in Paris and the National Cancer Institute in Bethesda, Maryland, announced the discovery and isolation of a virus that was causing this new disease. They named the virus <u>H</u>uman <u>I</u>mmunodeficiency <u>V</u>irus, or HIV, because the virus weakens a human's immune system, making it impossible for the system to fight other diseases. Scientists called the disease caused by the virus <u>A</u>cquired <u>I</u>mmune <u>D</u>eficiency <u>S</u>yndrome, or AIDS.

HIV is spread through contact with blood or body fluids from an infected person. This contact may take place during sexual activity, when using a contaminated hypodermic needle, or during a blood transfusion. Today there is little chance of being infected with HIV through a transfusion because all donated blood is carefully checked for contamination. HIV can also be transmitted from an infected mother to her baby during pregnancy.

No matter how HIV gets into the body, it is carried by the blood, where it finds the two specific white cells in the immune system it can infect. One of these is the helper T cell that controls the production of antibodies by the B cells and directs the attack of the killer T cells. The other cell is a macrophage, which is a large phagocyte that changes shape as it moves through the blood and body tissues, engulfing viruses and other foreign invaders. Scientists think infected macrophages are responsible for spreading HIV to other organs in the body, including the brain.

When someone is infected with HIV, the symptoms of AIDS may not show up right away. They may not appear for a few months, a few years, or even 12 years, which is an unusu-

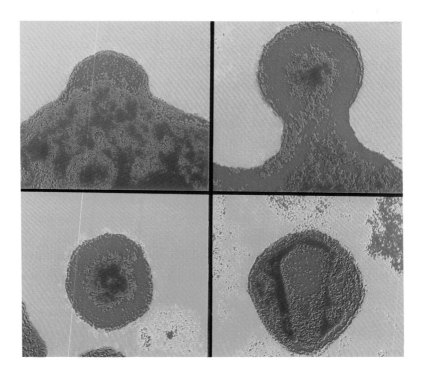

Formation of an HIV particle. The virus first appears (top left) as a small bump (red) on the surface of a cell. The virus then projects out (top right) and is eventually cut off from the cell. The newly released virus particle (bottom left) has a dense outer coat (red) that becomes elongated in the mature virus (bottom right).

ally long time for a virus to wait to act. In contrast, the measles virus moves fast. Two to three weeks after a person is infected, the symptoms appear. If the person doesn't get measles within this incubation period, it means antibodies have destroyed the invading virus.

The AIDS virus moves slowly, infecting one helper T cell or macrophage after another. Often, instead of killing a cell, the virus remains inside it and slowly duplicates itself. Sometimes the host cell is killed, and hundreds of viruses are released into the blood and other body fluids. Some HIVs may be destroyed by a person's antibodies, but at the same time, others are rapidly spreading the disease as they enter helper T cells and macrophages.

Slowly but surely this virus destroys the immune system. Before any symptoms appear, a blood test will be positive for AIDS because it will show the presence of antibodies that fight HIV. Eventually a person starts getting strange infections that can be treated, but that keep coming back. Finally the person develops what doctors call "full-blown AIDS." At this point the immune system is so damaged that the infections overwhelm the body and the person cannot survive.

There is no cure for AIDS, at least not yet. However, researchers all over the world are looking for and testing different drugs against HIV. Some drugs that stop the virus from reproducing, such as AZT, ddI, ddC, and d4T, have been developed. By slowing down the spread of HIV, these drugs help extend the lives of some people, but they do not cure them. The drugs are quite toxic and may cause serious side effects, such as liver and pancreas damage, anemia, and painful nerve irritation. The virus may also mutate and become resistant to these drugs within six to twelve months, which limits their usefulness. The drug thalidomide is an effective sleeping pill developed in the 1960s. But when used by pregnant women, thalidomide caused serious birth defects in their children. It was taken off the market, but now it is being tested as a possible drug to fight HIV. Another drug, called U-90,150, is an HIV killer in test tubes. It is being tested on a small group of volunteers with AIDS. Researchers are hopeful, but a drug that looks promising in a test tube may not necessarily work in the human body.

Genetic engineering is also being used in the search for a cure for AIDS. A technique that uses a harmless virus to carry an engineered gene into blood cells will soon be tested in animals. The gene has been developed to give the blood cells resistance to HIV. Some scientists are also experimenting with genetically engineered antibodies that would fight HIV within infected cells. Others are isolating and testing unusual compounds found in plants, fungi, insects, sea urchins, and other animals for possible virus-fighting properties.

Over 20 different AIDS vaccines are being tested on humans today. Most of the vaccines are made from tiny pieces of the outer coat of the virus or are synthetic copies of the coat. Researchers hope the immune system will identify these pieces as HIV and produce antibodies to fight the virus. Dr. Jonas Salk, who made the first polio vaccine using a killed polio virus, has developed a vaccine made with killed HIV, which may be more effective than a vaccine made with pieces of the virus. Researchers at Harvard Medical School are experimenting with a vaccine made from weakened live HIV. The vaccine has had good results in animal testing, but scientists say it will take 10 to 15 years of human trial testing before it can be given to all AIDS patients. One of the biggest problems in developing a vaccine to fight HIV is the ability of the virus to mutate very rapidly. By the time a person shows the symptoms of AIDS they may already be infected with hundreds or thousands of different strains of HIV, and each strain requires a slightly different antibody to attack it. Because of this, most scientists believe a general AIDS vaccine will not be available for many years.

With no vaccine and only AZT, ddI, ddC, and d4T approved by the Food and Drug Administration, many people infected with AIDS are desperately trying other things that might work against the disease. Acupuncture, old herbal

People gathered for a fund-raising walk for support services for AIDS sufferers. Inset: Dr. Jonas Salk, who is working on a vaccine that would cause people to develop antibodies to HIV in their blood before they are exposed to HIV infection.

remedies, diets high in special vitamins and minerals, and unusual foods have all been tried, but most of these treatments have not been very helpful. Some people in the United States use drugs from other countries, even though the drugs have not gone through the rigorous testing required for approval in the United States.

In April 1993, the World Health Organization reported that about 14 million people had been infected by the AIDS virus worldwide. It warned that the number of people with HIV could reach 40 million by the year 2000. In the United States, where more than one million people are known to be infected with HIV, AIDS is now one of the main causes of death in people between the ages of 20 and 40, and the rate is increasing each year in women and children.

6

PLANT VIRUSES

Tulip cultivators depend upon viruses for some of their new varieties. The bright yellow or white streaks in some of the red Dutch tulips, for example, were originally caused by a virus. But most plant viruses are not so welcome. Most, in fact, are so destructive they wipe out whole crops or cause deformed leaves, branches, fruit, or flowers. Some viruses stunt the growth of plants. Others destroy chlorophyll in the food-making cells, which mottles the leaves or turns them yellow. Some viruses kill plants quickly by destroying the transport tissues that carry water and food.

When wheat, corn, rice, and other important food crops are attacked by viruses, it can be a major disaster. Beginning in 1916, sugar beet crops around the world were almost wiped out when an epidemic of a viral disease called curly top lasted for 15 years. Sugar beets were the prime source of sugar, and the discovery of a resistant strain of sugar beet was found just in time to save the sugar industry. But the virus still causes serious diseases in tomatoes and beans.

Plants have no immune systems. Vaccines won't work because plants do not have white cells that can be stimulated into making antibodies. And without antibodies, there is no protection against viruses.

Like all other viruses, a plant virus must get into a cell before it can become active. But plant cells are surrounded by thick, tough walls that most viruses cannot penetrate. However, insects and mites, armed with their piercing or chewing or sucking mouth parts, can easily break through the cell walls. Aphids, leafhoppers, mealybugs, grasshoppers, mites, whiteflies, and beetles are the main distributors of viruses from infected plants to healthy plants. Underground, tiny roundworms called nematodes spread viruses as they chew on plant roots.

Some viruses can become part of an infected plant's seeds, and the seeds pass the virus along to the next generation of the plant. A few viruses infect pollen, and these are spread from plant to plant by pollinating insects.

Aphids attacking a plant. Aphids use their piercing jaws to drill tiny holes in the tough cell walls of a plant and get to the sap. As the aphids feed, viruses may be transmitted to the plant.

Farmers and gardeners may not realize how efficiently they spread viruses when they prune or trim plants. Pruning shears or saw blades used on an infected plant pick up the viruses and transfer them to the next plant they touch. This is why farmers and gardeners are advised to dip shears and saw blades into a disinfectant before moving from one plant to another when they prune.

The tobacco mosaic virus, which was the first plant disease discovered, can be spread by the simplest contact. The virus can live for more than 50 years in dried tobacco leaves, which end up in cigarettes and cigars. When handling a cigarette or cigar, a smoker's hand can be contaminated with the virus, and the virus can easily be passed on to the next plant the person touches.

Once infected by a virus, a plant is infected for life. There are no antiviral chemicals that can be sprayed or dusted on infected crops. The best advice is to immediately dig up and destroy infected plants.

The most successful war against plant virus diseases is being fought by plant breeders and genetic engineers. Every year, new varieties of plants are produced that are resistant to one or more of the diseases common to that species. Farmers can buy varieties of beans, tomatoes, and several other food plants that are now resistant to leaf spot and mosaic viruses. When a plant is advertised as "highly resistant to diseases," you know scientists have been at work against a virus.

The technique of moving genes around inside a plant and inserting new genes from another organism is commonly practiced today, but the big problem is finding the gene that will make the plant resistant to a specific disease. Researchers at Cornell University accidentally discovered that a certain gene from the tobacco mosaic virus, when placed in a tobacco plant, made the plant resistant to the virus. Although the researchers don't know how it works,

Technician checking test plants at a biotechnology lab. Through the use of selective breeding and genetic engineering, scientists are producing plants resistant to diseases. Plants with larger and more nutritious edible parts are also being developed.

they do know the gene stops the virus from reproducing in the plant and infecting it. The Cornell scientists also found the same gene was equally effective in protecting cucumbers against cucumber mosaic virus, a virus responsible for millions of dollars worth of damage to cucumbers each year.

Another gene has been identified that will provide resistance to four different viruses that cause diseases in squash, melons, and pumpkins, which have no natural resistance to the diseases. Papaya, which is a major food crop in tropical countries, has often been devastated by the papaya ring spot virus. Because papaya is a close relative of squash and melons, scientists are hopeful that when this gene is transferred into a papaya plant, it will produce immunity

51

against the ring spot virus. The gene transfer technique provides a permanent fix because once a new gene has been put into a plant, it becomes part of the plant's DNA and is passed on to its offspring.

Viruses are not always harmful to plants. They can also be beneficial. The case of the processionary caterpillars is a good example. The caterpillars' name comes from their habit of following one another in an unbroken, head-to-tail chain as they crawl from branch to branch eating pine needles. When billions of processionary caterpillars were destroying 5,000 acres (2,000 hectares) of pine forest in southern France, scientists were asked to find a way to stop them. The scientists knew they had found the right weapon when they discovered one specific virus that can infect and kill this caterpillar without harming any other form of life. In the laboratory, they

A viral insecticide being sprayed on a cotton field. The virus used in a viral spray is harmless to every living thing except the target pest.

raised processionary caterpillars and infected them with the virus. When the caterpillars died, they were ground up, mixed with water, and sprayed over the forest. It wasn't long before the caterpillars that were dining on the forest became infected with the virus and died, and the forest was saved.

In tropical countries, millions of people depend upon a basic diet of cassava, a root crop that provides starch and tapioca. But farmers were always battling a caterpillar called the cassava hornworm. Now science has given these people a simple recipe for a spray that will save their cassava crops. A farmer needs to collect only a dozen hornworms that are infected by a virus. They are easy to find because an infected hornworm swells up like a little balloon. When the infected hornworms are ground up and added to water, the farmer has enough solution to spray and destroy the caterpillars on two and a half acres (one hectare).

A hundred years ago, the American chestnut tree was one of the most important trees in the hardwood forests of the eastern United States. It was also a beautiful shade tree around homes, and it produced delicious nuts. Its durable, rot-resistant wood was used for telephone poles, railroad ties, shingles, paneling, and fine furniture. Unfortunately, about four billion of these chestnut trees have been killed by a fungus. The tree is almost extinct, but it may be saved by researchers who have developed a synthetic virus that kills the fungus. The scientists have applied to the U.S. Department of Agriculture for permission to begin greenhouse and field trials of the synthetic virus on American chestnut trees.

Genetic engineers are trying to create plants that will work like animals in their ability to make antibodies against their most common diseases. The mosaic virus, for example, that infects tobacco and other crops, has been injected into laboratory mice. A mouse's immune system reacts to this foreign virus by making antibodies against it. The next step, which sounds almost like science fiction, is to find the gene in the mouse that contains the blueprint for the antibody and then transfer the gene into the plant. Once that coded information is in place, the plant will be able to make its own antibodies against mosaic virus. Research has certainly come a long way since Dimitry Ivanovski first filtered infected tobacco juice in 1892.

7

THE EVER-CHANGING VIRUS

Viruses are constantly mutating, and some of the mutants have produced devastating diseases in this century. Many of these diseases originated in tropical regions where there are great concentrations and varieties of plants and animals to host a large variety of viruses. Each new disease probably infected and killed people even before it was recognized and identified. AIDS was first recorded in Africa in 1959. Africa was also where Lassa fever was identified in 1969. The Lassa fever virus spreads easily from rats to people and person to person in blood and urine. There is no cure or vaccine for Lassa fever. Some scientists believe the disease has remained in West Africa, at least for now, because the virus kills so quickly that infected people do not have time to leave the area and spread the disease.

In Africa in 1976, another dangerous virus was detected when it killed half the people it infected in a small village in Sudan. Later in 1976, the disease, called Ebola fever, swept through 50 villages in Zaire and killed 90 percent of the infected people. Today Ebola fever has almost disappeared, but scientists are certain the virus is still around. It may just be living in some animal host waiting for the right conditions to cause another epidemic.

In the late 1980s, farmers in England were astonished when their normally placid, quiet cows became agitated. Some of the cows became aggressive while others became quite fearful of people. As this strange disease progressed, the cows got weaker and weaker. Finally they couldn't even stand up, and soon died. In a span of five years, tens of thousands of cows died from this new plague, which newspapers called the "mad cow disease." Cats were the next victims, and then some animals in the London Zoo also developed this weird behavior before they died. Scientists believe this mad cow disease was caused by one of the slow viruses that grows for long periods in the nervous system before it produces symptoms. In humans, diseases such as Parkinson's, Alzheimer's, and several other diseases of the nervous system may also be caused by slow viruses.

Viruses have always hitched rides, but with modern transportation, viruses travel faster and farther on people and products to places where they have never been seen before. In the summer of 1993, a mysterious, flulike disease struck the Navajo people in an area of the United States called Four Corners, where the borders of Utah, Colorado, Arizona, and New Mexico meet. Epidemiologists, who collect statistics about epidemics, quickly traced the disease to a virus carried by deer mice. It turned out to be the Hantaan virus, which is spread to humans when they breathe in fine particles of dried mouse droppings that are carried in the air. Hantaan is an ancient disease, once known as hemorrhagic fever in China. It is now named for the Hantaan River in Korea, a country where the disease is a major health problem. The virus first came to the United States after the Korean War in the 1950s, when some soldiers returned home infected with the disease. However, there was no record of an outbreak of the disease until 1993 in Four Corners. Other viral diseases, such as St. Louis encephalitis, dengue fever, and

Lab technologist preparing a slide of tissue taken from a person infected with the Hantaan virus. Because Hantaan, the disease caused by this virus, is rare in the United States, the first deaths in 1993 were considered a mystery.

AIDS, were spread in recent years in this "viral traffic" that transfers viruses from animals to humans, from rural areas to cities, and from nation to nation.

As viruses travel around the world, they mutate and appear in new disguises. They can invade new organisms or become more deadly and contagious. Diphtheria is a serious, infectious disease that has been around for centuries and is caused by a poison made by a type of bacteria. But in 1951, scientists discovered that the bacteria themselves are harmless. It is only when the bacteria are infected by a certain virus that they produce the poison that causes diphtheria.

Streptococci are common bacteria that live in most people's throats and sometimes cause strep throat infections. But if the strep bacteria are invaded by a virus, the bacteria produce a strong poison that changes them from relatively harmless bacteria into deadly ones, called severe group A strep. These deadly bacteria first began causing an infectious disease in the United States in 1987. The disease almost disappeared in 1991 and 1992, but in 1993 it struck over 10,000 people in the United States. Scientists predict at least twice as many people will be infected in the next few years.

Dr. Robert T. Schooley, who heads the infectious diseases department at the University of Colorado, has said, "Life is competition—and we compete with microbes." And that is the challenge. In the competition against viruses, there is still so much to learn about these ever-changing invaders.

GLOSSARY

AIDS (Acquired Immune Deficiency Syndrome): a deadly, infectious disease caused by a virus that attacks and destroys the immune system, resulting in the body's inability to resist other infections.

antibody: a protein produced by certain white blood cells that attacks foreign substances in the body.

bacteriologist: a scientist who studies and experiments with bacteria.

bacteriophage: a virus that attacks and lives in a certain bacterium.

B cell: a type of lymphocyte that produces antibodies; part of the human immune system.

chromosome: a tiny particle in the nucleus of a cell that carries the genes.

DNA (deoxyribonucleic acid): an acid found in the nucleus of a living cell; contains the codes needed to build proteins and carries the genetic information about an organism.

electron microscope: a microscope that uses electron rays instead of light rays to produce very high magnification.

gene: the minute part of a chromosome that holds genetic information and determines a specific characteristic of an organism.

genetic engineering: the alteration of genetic material in an organism; involves the transfer of DNA from one cell to another.

helper T cell: a T cell that activates B cells to release antibodies and killer T cells to destroy certain cells.

HIV (Human Immunodeficiency Virus): the virus that causes AIDS.

immune system: a system of antibodies and white blood cells that recognizes, attacks, and destroys foreign invaders that enter the body.

immunity: resistance to a disease or posion.

interferon: a protein produced by cells infected by a virus; it protects similar cells from infection by the same virus.

killer T cell: a large T cell that attacks and kills certain infected cells so the infectious material can be exposed to attack by antibodies.

lymphocyte: a type of white blood cell that is primarily responsible for the development of immunity; includes B cells and T cells.

macrophage: a large phagocyte that helps the immune system by engulfing foreign invaders.

memory cell: a B cell or T cell that has been exposed to a foreign substance and can instantly respond to the same invader at a later time.

molecule: the smallest particle into which an element can be divided without changing its properties.

mutant: a new variety of animal or plant carrying a gene or chromosome that has undergone mutation.

mutation: a change within a gene or chromosome resulting in a new characteristic that is inherited.

phagocyte: a type of white blood cell that engulfs and destroys foreign invaders.

protein: a substance containing nitrogen; the major structural building block of animal and plant cells.

RNA (ribonucleic acid): an acid found in living cells and which takes the place of DNA in some viruses.

T cell: a type of lymphocyte that regulates the response of the immune system or kills certain types of cells.

vaccine: a substance made from killed or weakened viruses or bacteria used to inoculate a person in order to prevent a disease and produce immunity to it; a vaccine works by causing the body to develop antibodies to the disease organisms.

virus: a disease-producing particle composed of genetic material covered with a protein coat; a virus can only reproduce in a living cell.

X-ray crystallography: the study of the structure of crystals by means of producing images created by high-powered X rays.

FURTHER READING

Aaseng, Nathan. *The Disease Fighters*. Minneapolis: Lerner, 1987.

———. *The Common Cold and the Flu*. New York: Watts, 1992.

Greenberg, Lorna. *AIDS: How It Works in the Body*. New York: Watts, 1992.

Hyde, Margaret, and Elizabeth Forsyth. *Know About AIDS*. New York: Walker, 1990.

Jaret, Peter. "Viruses," *National Geographic*, July 1994.

Nourse, Alan E. *Your Immune System*. New York: Watts, 1989.

———. *Lumps, Bumps, and Rashes: A Look at Kids' Diseases*. New York: Watts, 1990.

———. *The Virus Invaders*. New York: Watts, 1992.

Thompson, Paul D. *The Virus Realm*. New York: Lippincott, 1968.

Tomlinson, Michael. *Jonas Salk*. Vero Beach, Fla.: Rourke, 1993.

INDEX